Carnoustie
in old picture postca.

by Annie L. Thompson

European Library ZALTBOMMEL/THE NETHERLANDS

Cover picture:
This view along the High Street, looking west is postmarked 1920 and appears to have been taken the previous year. The shops on the near left have now gone to make way for the Public Library. The Post Card Shop on the right may have been the original source of many of the cards which make up this book.

About the author:
Annie Thompson is a journalist whose interest in her home town's history goes back many years. As a member of Carnoustie Twinning Association she has undertaken research for a historical association in Maule, France, the town which has been linked with Carnoustie since 1992. For several years she has taught a course in Local History for Carnoustie Community Education.

BACK IN TIME

GB ISBN 90 288 1146 x
© 1998 European Library – Zaltbommel/The Netherlands

Introduction

The town of Carnoustie was founded just over 200 years ago, but the name comes from the ancient language of the Picts and most likely means Hill of the Fir Trees. Not to be taken seriously are a couple of fanciful nineteenth century explanations. Because the sandhills on which the town is built yielded a large number of ancient stone coffins or cists dating back to the Bronze Age the early builders of Carnoustie assumed they were all casualties of a battle buried in a 'Cairn o'Hosts'. Some Carnoustie inhabitants used to point out to visitors the many rookeries in the trees on the higher part of the town with the solemn explanation that the name derived from 'Craws' Nestie'!

Before 1797 Carnoustie was a large farm in the parish of Barry. A document of 1573 states that a man named Fairney held both Carnoustie and Grange of Barry, paying feu to Arbroath Abbey. The farm had several more owners until in 1792 it was bought by Major William Philip, who, with his neighbour to the west, David Hunter of Pitskelly, conceived the idea of building a village, which they called Taymouth Feus.

The first feu was taken up by Thomas Lowson, a loomwright from Barry. Legend says he was making his way between the weavers' hamlets of Inverpeffer and Buddon Ness on a warm summer's day. Stopping to rest halfway he fell asleep. His dream that he had a cottage on that spot was so vivid that he awoke determined to make it come true.

The sandy soil of his patch turned out to be so fertile that even the twig Thomas used as a dibble while planting cabbages took root and grew into a tree, a proof which encouraged others to settle at Taymouth Feus.

There had been an earlier plan for a village just east of Carnoustie when in 1670 George Maule, Third Earl of Panmure, had plans prepared for a harbour between the fishing villages of Westhaven and Easthaven to provide shelter for ships waiting for high tide so they could proceed up the Tay to Dundee. Mauleshaven actually appears on a map of that period, but its construction was postponed when James VII and II was forced to abdicate. George Maule devoted his fortune to the hopeless cause of restoring King James, and Mauleshaven was never built.

In 1807 Major Philip sold Carnoustie to George Kinloch, MP for Dundee. Mr. Kinloch planned a grid of streets, changed the name of the settlement to Carnoustie and opened a brickworks, which, with a quarry owned by David Hunter at Pitskelly, supplied the building materials for the early feuars, who were mostly handloom weavers.

As many of them were members of the two Secession Churches George Kinloch in 1810 allowed both congregations to build churches in Carnoustie. One of these is still in use as

Erskine United Free Church. Mr. Kinloch also encouraged a baker, shoemender and grocer to set up shop.

As early as 1810 a family from Kirriemuir took summer lodgings in Carnoustie in order to benefit from the sea air. The opening in 1838 of the Dundee/Arbroath Railway encouraged professional and business families to settle, and brought in more holidaymakers. It was at this time that the village, until then bounded on the east by the Lochty Burn, extended into the neighbouring parish of Panbride.

Golf had been played informally on Barry Links since the sixteenth century. Now, in the early 1840s, golf clubs were established and the first specially-constructed golf courses laid out. Carnoustie became a Burgh in 1889, with a Provost and Town Council. Money was raised to purchase a large section of the Links for golf and other leisure activities. The remainder of the Links, stretching to Buddon Ness, was bought by the War Department and Barry and Buddon Camps were established in 1897.

The Town Council encouraged tourism, claiming Carnoustie as the 'Brighton of the North'. They and their successors sought the latest visitor attractions to add to the natural advantages of five miles of sandy beach, attractive scenery and one of the sunniest climates in the British Isles.

At a time when few people had the use of a telephone there was a huge demand for postcards from holidaymakers, soldiers, and indeed the local residents.

Now these cards tell the story of the town that grew from a twig.

I wish to acknowledge the help of Andrew Reid, David Torrie, David Hovell, Rev. Colin Caskie, Rev. Ian Forrester and Reg Cunningham, who kindly allowed me to borrow from their collections the postcards which make up this book.

1 As Thomas Lowson planted cabbage seedlings in his new garden in the spring of 1798, passers-by on the road from Barry to Westhaven shook their heads. Nothing could grow so close to the sea, they said, but they were proved wrong. Not only did Thomas's cabbages thrive, but the twig he had cut from a willow tree to use as a dibble and had left stuck in the earth took root and sprouted leaves. Two hundred years later Tam's Dibble, now a venerable crack-willow, still flourishes, grown much larger than it appears in this picture.

Tammas Lowson's Dibble, Carnoustie.

2 The caption on this card repeats a local legend, now discounted. Although Hector Boece of Panbride, writing in the sixteenth century, described a defeat by Malcolm II in the early eleventh century of a Danish raiding party led by a prince named Camus, records of that period make no mention of such a battle or of anyone named Camus. In fact, relations between Malcolm and the Danish King Sueno were amicable. The cross, which is from around 1000 AD, may mark the site of an early church building. A cist found near it by Sir Patrick Maule in 1620, containing human bones and an urn, and assumed by him to be the grave of Camus, was probably a Beaker burial from many centuries BC. The cross was moved to its present position from lower down Downie Hill during landscaping in 1853.

The Camus Cross, Panmure.—Marks the grave of Camus, the Leader of the Danes. who was slain in the retreat from the Battle of Barry in 1010.

3 Panmure House, built in 1664 by George Maule, second Earl of Panmure, using stones from the old castle and from a quarry on the estate, was said to have been cursed by an old woman whose cottage was pulled down to clear the site. She prophesied that within three hundred years the stones would return to the earth whence they were dug. In 1953 the house and estate, by that time the property of the Earl of Dalhousie, were sold to pay death duties. As no use could be found for the mansion – now in disrepair – it was demolished in 1955 and the stones used to infill the quarry. The stable block and chapel survive.

Panmure House

4 In 1715 James, 4th Earl of Panmure, and his brother, Harry Maule of Kelly, rode out of Panmure with an army they had raised to assist their nephew, the Earl of Mar, in his support of the cause of the Pretender, James Stuart, against George of Hanover, who had been chosen to succeed Queen Anne. Earl James ordered the gates to be locked behind them, never to be re-opened until a Stuart king should sit on the British throne. Almost three hundred years later the gates remain locked, while the drive that led from them and the house itself no longer exist. Six weeks after his triumphal departure the Earl returned to Panmure from the field of Sherriffmuir disguised as beggar. He had been taken prisoner, and then rescued by his brother Harry and a servant, Henry Fairlie.

5 Knowing Panmure would be watched, the Earl and Fairlie left their horses at New-bigging, donned rags and continued on foot. The Earl's wife, Margaret, concealed him in a secret room at Panmure until she could arrange for him to leave the country. As he rode away towards Easthaven where a fishing boat waited to take him to a ship lying off Montrose, which would carry him to exile in France, Margaret watched until he was out of sight, and later had this memorial placed on the spot. The Earl never returned to Scotland.

Margaret, through the influence of her father, the Duke of Hamilton, was permitted to remain in Panmure House, although the estate was confiscated and sold off to the York Building Company. Margaret set up a hand-spinning business and before her death in 1732 had succeeded in buying back part of the estate. The purchase was completed some years later by Harry Maule's son, William.

6   Carnoustie children learn the points of the compass by reciting, 'North to the Monument, South to the sea, East to Arbroath and West to Dundee'. The Panmure Testimonial, also called the Live and Let Live Monument, was erected by the grateful tenants of William Ramsay Maule, Baron Panmure. A sympathetic and fair-minded landlord, during the famine years of the 1820s he excused his farmer tenants from paying rent. When times improved he refused to accept the back rents he was offered, so the money was used to build this tower on Downie Hill, one mile from Panmure House. Completed in 1839, and 106 feet high, it contains a stair leading to a viewing platform. The monument was damaged during the storm of December 1879 which destroyed the Tay Rail Bridge. When it was repaired an urn was placed on the pinnacle in memory of three Panmure House servants who perished in the Tay Bridge disaster.

Panmure Monument, Carnoustie

7   The earliest lighthouse on Buddon Ness was a seventeenth-century wooden structure on a wheeled platform which could be moved whenever the shifting of the Tay sandbanks made this necessary. An eighteenth-century stone tower was made obsolete by further shifting of the sands, so when these two lighthouses were erected in 1868, it was cut down to form part of the light-keeper's house seen in this picture. Still further sand movement meant that twenty years later the Lower Light, a 65-foot high, 440 ton structure had to be moved on rollers. At the rate of five feet per hour, it took a month to relocate it 160 feet to the north-east.

Later sand drift has made the lights redundant, but they remain in repair in case they should again be needed.

Buddon Ness Lighthouses, Barry Camp

8   The Upper Mill is the only one left of four by the Barry Burn. There has been a mill here since the sixteenth century, but this building dates from 1815 when the previous mill was destroyed by fire. A working business until 1984, it has been restored by the National Trust for Scotland and is open to the public, who can see oats being ground. This is done for demonstration only, and the meal is used for animal food, as under present-day health regulations it is not considered suitable for human consumption. The bridge to the left of the picture is older than the town of Carnoustie. Built in 1777, it carries the ancient road which once linked Barry and Panbride, and which has never been paved. Just above the keystone of the bridge is a carving of a man ploughing.

THE UPPER MILL, CARNOUSTIE

9   Carnoustie Bay, seen in a 70-year-old picture, was once known as Barry Sands. Here in 1659 three Forfar witches, Helen Guthrie, Isobel Shyrie and Elspeth Alexander, met on St. James's Night, 18th July, with three Barry witches and the Devil. They built a fire and brought about the stranding of a ship on Barry Sands, then parted after making arrangements to meet again at Hallowe'en. The Forfar witches were brought to trial in 1661. Guthrie and Shyrie were executed. Alexander was released. Neither the Barry witches nor the man who took the part of the Devil were ever identified.

General View of the Beach. Carnoustie

10 These eighteenth-century weavers' cottages with stone-slate roofs were formerly thatched. They still stand, now much modernised. The old church of Barry, visible to the right of the dormer-windowed house, was demolished in the 1960s. The bank on which the houses stand is the old shore line. Barry, once called Fothermuref or Fettermore, is now over a mile inland, but a prophecy attributed to Thomas the Rhymer states: 'The braes o' Fettermore ha'e been a guid ship shore. The braes o' Fettermore again sall be a guid ship shore.' Recently there are signs that the sand dunes which lie between Barry and the Firth of Tay are being eroded.

BARRY VILLAGE.

11 This view of the west bank of the Barry Burn was taken in the early 1890s. None of the buildings seen here exists today. The white house with the dovecote was the Inn of Barry, now replaced by a 1930s bungalow. The old parish school and dominie's house were demolished in 1896, the pupils having been transferred some years earlier to the former Free Church School. A church hall built on the site in 1902 has now also been taken down and a garden has been planted in its place. The church was knocked down in 1965, but as there was no means of getting through the churchyard to remove the rubble, it remains piled up there. Buried under it are a number of mediaeval gravestones, recycled as floor paving when the church was renovated in 1820.

At Barry

Valentines Series

12   Oddly, this view taken from the same spot as the last, facing in the other direction, has altered very little in over a hundred years. The house on the left is the gate lodge of Ravensby, built in 1854. Barry post office and shop now stand where this picture shows a tree stump on the right. The Barry Burn once took a turn to the east just below the bridge. The road through the village still follows the burn's old course, with a sharp bend in front of Barry Church. During the eighteenth century David Moram, the farmer of Gedhall, straightened out the burn by digging a new course for it, in an attempt to prevent his fields being flooded. Although it is nowadays heavily embanked, the burn still makes the occasional effort to return to its old bed.

Barry Bridge.

13 The Dundee-Arbroath Railway, opened in 1838, encouraged both industry and tourism. A suburb grew up on the east side of the Lochty Burn on the lands of Newton of Panbride. Large houses were built for the families of Dundee professional and business men who found it convenient to commute to the city by rail, while their wives and families had the benefit of sea-air, away from the smoke of the Dundee factories. Unusually for Scotland, a number of these house-sites were on 99-year lease instead of the more usual feu, so this area used to be known as the Ninety-nines. Motor transport came later, but by 1905 automobiles were being built in Carnoustie at George Anderson's iron works. The 'Dalhousie' car was built to order. When Mr. Anderson retired in 1912 the car-building was moved to Arbroath.

The Railway Crossing, Carnoustie

14 Golf was played on Barry Links as early as 1500, but there was no formal course. In 1838 Bobby Millar, a keen golfer, came from St. Andrews to settle in Carnoustie. Along with a schoolmaster called Mr. Spankie, he set about organising golf clubs at Barry and Carnoustie. David Hunter of Pitskelly got Robert Chambers, the Edinburgh publisher and golfing enthusiast, to help lay out on Carnoustie Links a six-hole course with the first tee where the Bruce Hotel is now. From 1843 onwards several golf clubs were established in the town and the golf course was improved and extended as the reputation of Carnoustie's links and native golfers grew .

Links Parade, Carnoustie ·

Valentines Series

15   In 1889 Carnoustie became a Burgh with a Town Council and a Provost, David McCorquodale, a bank agent. A town crest was devised, showing a tree to represent Thomas Lowson's Dibble and a nest of birds - the 'craw's nestie' pun on the town's name. The Latin motto meaning 'the sign is favourable' refers to the encouraging of the early settlers by the sprouting of the Dibble. Carnoustie was eventually granted a coat of arms in 1953, when the new motto was chosen, 'Stay the Course'.

At the First Hole, Carnoustie.

RELIABLE SERIES

16   Here are two of Carnoustie's lost landmarks. Dalhousie Golf Club, built in 1864, was demolished in 1998 to make way for timeshare apartments. The Links Bandstand, for almost a hundred years a popular venue for outdoor concerts, was removed in the 1970s after it became a target for vandals. Edwardian holidaymakers are seen on a Sunday afternoon enjoying the music of the Burgh Band. The bathchair is a reminder that Carnoustie was popular with convalescents seeking sea air to aid their recovery.

The Bandstand, Carnoustie

17 Edwardian spectators are here watching a match on the Ladies' Course at Links Parade. When the Ladies' Club was founded in 1873 it was thought that women lacked the skill and stamina for anything more than six short holes. Women took to the game with great enthusiasm and when the fashion changes of the twentieth century relieved them from the restrictions of whalebone corsets, long skirts and boater hats they soon showed they were equal to any course. The Ladies' Course was then turned into a putting green.

The Links, Carnoustie.

18 For over a hundred years for around 30,000 men Carnoustie has meant each year not golf and seaside, but military training. Fox Maule, Baron Panmure and later Earl of Dalhousie, was Secretary of State for War at the time of Crimea. He saw the need for well-trained volunteer regiments, and from the 1860s onward allowed Buddon Ness to be used informally for artillery practice. In the late 1880s the area was bought by the War Department and a permanent training ground established in 1897. This picture shows some of the earliest users, men of the Forfarshire Volunteer Artillery with a field battery.

19 The Soldiers' Home, constructed entirely of corrugated iron, provided the men camped under canvas with off-duty refreshments, recreation and concert entertainments which were attended also by local residents. It was one of a number founded by Miss Williamina Davidson, a Sister of the Order of St. John of Jerusalem. It was demolished several years ago when the new building complex was erected at what is now Barry-Buddon Camp. On the left of this picture is one of the farm cottages of Cowbyres, an old farm swallowed up by the training ground.

"Field Batteries," at Buddon Camp

Soldiers' Home, Barry Camp

20 Apart from the Soldiers' Home the Barry and Buddon Camps had no permanent buildings. All the camp activities took place in the open air, including cooking with field kitchens. The bush hats, adopted by regiments who served in Africa, suggest that these men lined up with their billy-cans may be Sappers of the Lanarkshire Royal Engineers Volunteers. Rations were basic. It's probable that the barrels contained salt herrings or salt pork.

21 Barry and Buddon Camps had their own post office – open only during the camping season – in an outbuilding attached to a farmhouse just north of Barry Station. Here men of a Highland regiment are reading their mail. All the men slept in bell tents like these seen here. Many early Carnoustie postcards, not only of the camp, but of the town and beach, bear messages to the families of men camped at Barry and Buddon. Early postcards often have printed on them the advice that any written messages are for inland postage only.

"The Kitchen," Barry Camp

Valentines Series

Letters, Barry Camp

61458. (V)

22 The date 16th August 1916 is written on the back of this card showing a cavalry regiment striking camp. We can see that a wing has been added to the Soldiers' Home to cope with the added volume of men coming here for wartime training. Horses were still an important part of the army's equipment. They could haul guns and other loads over ground impassible to motor vehicles. Army horses were boarded during the winter months by farmers all over Angus, who had the use of the animals in return for providing fodder and veterinary care. Each spring the horses were collected in herds and driven to Barry. Here a train is seen waiting for the men, perhaps to carry them on the first part of a journey to the battlefields.

23 In 1914 Bombardier George Kirtley of the Highland Brigade Durham Regiment sent this card to tell his mother in Durham he had arrived safely at Buddon Camp and was in good spirits, although he had been on guard duty during the night and so was feeling rather sleepy. Perhaps it reassured her to know that the men marched each Sunday to Barry Church. Here they are returning over the railway at Barry Station, led by a pipe band and escorted by local children in their Sunday clothes. The field on the left appears to have been planted with potatoes, a crop much grown around Carnoustie, with the War Department a main buyer of the produce.

Barry Camp.

Coming from Church, Barry Camp.

24   This handsome Italian-style building was erected in 1869 for the City of Glasgow Bank, which had an agency in Carnoustie from 1856. After this bank's failure in 1887 the premises were occupied by the North of Scotland Bank and then up to the present by the Clydesdale Bank. This card was sent in 1907 to Miss Annie Keates, Leek, Staffordshire, inviting her to come to Carnoustie for a holiday . The writer, who signed only with an initial, added 'and bring anybody else that would like to come. We will find room somewhere'.

North of Scotland Bank, Carnoustie   Valentines Series

25 Panbride Manse, built in 1864, is now a private house re-named Panbride Manor. It is said some of the stones used in building it came from the cell of the monk appointed in mediaeval times by the Abbot of Arbroath to minister to the parish. In later times Panbride was served by three generations of the Trail family, the Rev. Robert Trail from 1717, his son Robert and grandson David until 1844. Two generations of Caesars, James and John, then served until 1938. David Trail's sister Agnes became an Ursuline nun. As Sister Agnes Xavier she founded St. Margaret's Convent School in Edinburgh.

Panbride Manse, Carnoustie.

26 After the Disruption the break-away Free Church of Panbride worshipped first in a barn and then in a wooden building at Westhaven Farm until in 1854 the Earl of Dalhousie gave them stone from his quarry to build a church on the Gallowlaw, where malefactors had once been hanged. The church was damaged by fire and rebuilt in 1887 to a design by James Mclaren. After the Reunification of 1929 it was known as Newton Panbride Parish Church. Now united with the former Panbride Church, the congregation, known as Carnoustie Panbride Parish Church, use both buildings, worshipping in the older church during three months in summer and the rest of the year here.

Panbride United Free Church, Carnoustie

27   Panbride House was built in 1856 for John Dickson, owner of the bleachfield works established in the early 1840s. Linen yarn was treated with vitriol from Tennant's Works at the other end of Carnoustie, then hung on wires to whiten in the sun before being passed on to be woven at Smieton's Works. This artificial lake with water drawn from the Craigmill Burn served both as ornamental feature and as a reservoir for the bleachworks. A mill lade brought water from Craigmill Dam, behind the house to turn the wheel which powered the yarn processing machinery. The remains of this boat can still be seen, and the descendants of the swans introduced by John Dickson nest here each year. The former bleachworks area is now a small industrial estate.

Panbride House, Carnoustie   Valentines Series

28 This picture must have been taken just after the Municipal Buildings, designed by James Bruce, were erected in 1898, as just visible on the left is part of the shop of Jane Paris, a game dealer. The following year this was replaced by the block of shops and flats called Paris House. The street between was Point Lane, now called Lochty Street. Just behind the Municipal Buildings stood the Commercial Inn, formerly Point House, which was older than Carnoustie. It's said it was at the Point that Thomas Lowson purchased the ale, bread and cheese which he ate just before his historic dream among the sandhills. The Commercial Inn was demolished to provide the Municipal Buildings with a car park.

Municipal Buildings, Carnoustie

29   Postmarked 1901, this card shows the newly-built Paris House. The cottages on the right were demolished some years later to make way for Strachan's Garage. At one time all of Carnoustie's main thoroughfare was called Dundee Street, but later the eastern section was re-named High Street. Note that the roadway is unpaved. It was quite usual for early postcards to have the message written on the same side as the picture, with on the back the address only. Like many others of this period, this card was produced by Valentine Ltd. of Dundee.

Printed by Valentine, Ltd., Dundee.

Would you please mention what is Miss Thomson's number in Glasgow when next you write.
Yours,
Alex.

Dundee Street, Carnoustie

30 The Dalhousie Hotel in Church Street was famous for its fish dinners. It was extended in the 1850s by its owner, Miss Mary Watson. It was the first hotel in the town to install bathrooms, at a time when these were unusual in all but the most luxurious of private homes. This card is postmarked 1907. The hotel was demolished some years ago, following a fire. A courtyard group of villas and flats has recently been erected on its site. Carnoustie still has a Dalhousie Hotel, a former doctor's residence, originally called Dalhousie Villa, in the High Street.

DALHOUSIE HOTEL, CARNOUSTIE,

A. BARNSON, PROPRIETOR.

DALHOUSIE HOTEL

31   The original Bruce's Hotel was in Church Street. In 1892 Miss Mary Bruce built a very large hotel on the Links. It featured 'Large Dining and Drawing Rooms, Private Parlours, Smoking and large Billiard Room with every Modern Convenience'. The Bruce Hotel, as it was later known, was visited by many celebrities, including film star Bob Hope. Closed in 1982, it has been converted into flats. The small building on the right was the hotel laundry. Behind it can be seen the steeple of the old parish church.

Bruce's Hotel, Carnoustie   Valentines Series

32 Built in 1840, the Railway Hotel was later renamed the Panmure Arms by permission of Lord Panmure, who later became Earl of Dalhousie. For many years now it has been the Station Hotel, but its recently-constructed function rooms, built where this picture shows a conservatory, have the name of The Panmure Suite. The donkey cart seen in this picture may be bringing from the beach a load of seaweed, much used by Carnoustie gardeners as a fertiliser. The road is an unpaved sandy track, as were many of Carnoustie's side streets, well into the twentieth century.

Panmure Arms and Station Hotel, Carnoustie

33 A later view shows the name Station Hotel. A line of George Ness's motor taxi-cabs awaits train arrivals, with a horse-drawn cab also available for anyone preferring more traditional transport. The Carnoustie Coal and Lime Company's depot on the left has nowadays been replaced by the Tesco supermarket. Prior to 1890 this was the site of the Lochty Preserve Works which supplied the military with canned carrots and parsnips. Carnoustie was then famous for the carrots which grew well in sandy soil. The works was moved to Thistle Street, where it still functions today as Mackay's Preserves, making marmalade and also a range of jams from local soft fruit.

STATION ROAD, CARNOUSTIE

34 Carnoustie Public School, designed by James McLaren, was opened in 1878, under headmaster James Nicholson. Fees ranged from tenpence a month for infants to one shilling and fourpence for Standard Six. Where more than four children from the same family were in school together, the eldest was admitted free. Before the Education Act of 1872 Carnoustie had several church and private schools, and the Panmure Institute, which offered half-time education to juvenile employees of Smieton's Linen Works. Until 1924 the Public School provided education up to Standard Six. Scholars wishing to continue further had to travel to Arbroath or Broughty Ferry. After that date a three-year secondary course was available.

35 The church in this picture has twice been dismantled and rebuilt, moving one mile further east. In 1773 the Antiburgher Seceders built a church at Barry. In 1810 they took it apart and re-erected it in Carnoustie in the Rye Park, later Thistle Street, where it was called the Red Kirk from the colour of its sandstone. By 1873 the congregation, now United Presbyterian, had grown so much the stones were again removed and augmented to build this larger church designed by Robert Baldie in Dundee Street. After a split in the congregation in 1930 it was sold and converted into a cinema. It is nowadays a lounge bar and snooker club.

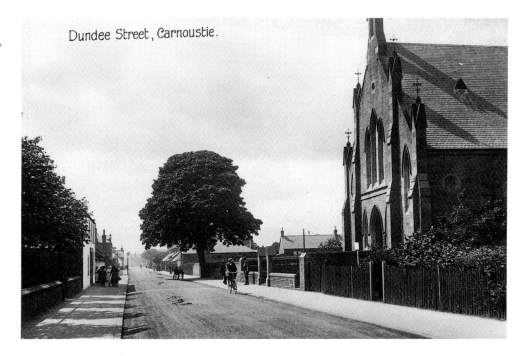

Dundee Street, Carnoustie.

36 A three-day bazaar on Carnoustie Links in 1898 raised £2,500 towards the £6,000 needed to build a new parish church. Designed by McGregor Chalmers, the church was consecrated in 1902. By heroic effort, it was by 1910 cleared of debt. To keep down the cost, the spire was omitted. After 1902 the former church building across the street became the town's first cinema. It was then bought in 1919 by the Territorial Army and used as a drill hall. By 1939 it had become so unsafe it was demolished. A plan to mark the 100th anniversary of its founding by building the postponed tower and transferring the clock to it was frustrated by the outbreak of the Second World War.

37 This interior of Carnoustie Parish Church shows its fine organ, the pulpit and the font. The church seats 1,100 and has some fine stained glass, including a War Memorial Window, installed in 1923, which is the work of two women artists, Margaret Chilton and Marjorie Kemp. At the time of its building there was a suggestion that the new church should have a new name. St. Columba's was suggested, but this was not taken up. The rounded arches seen in this picture show that the church is Norman in style.

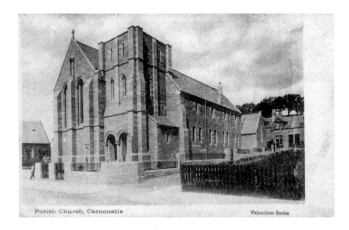

Parish Church, Carnoustie

Valentines Series

Parish Church, Carnoustie

38 Carnoustie High Street has changed little in the ninety years since this picture was taken. The trees have gone and electricity has replaced the gas street lighting, but the shop on the left is still a baker's and the shop with the sunblind is again a wine merchant's. Between the two was Carnoustie's original post office. The post office later moved to a shop in Dundee Street next to the police station, and then, in 1934, to purpose-built premises in Queen Street. Note the small boy on the left is wearing a kilt. Gas street lighting was installed in Carnoustie as early as 1856 through the efforts of William Balfour, who raised the money by giving, in the Red Kirk, a series of lectures on local history, charging his audience one shilling per head.

39 Further along the High Street an errand boy carries a covered basket past the YMCA building, built in 1854. The excavation of its foundations uncovered several ancient graves with bones in stone coffins. Unlike others found in the area these skeletons were laid full length with their feet pointing east, which suggests they were from the Christian period, possibly 7th or 8th century AD. So many cist burials have been found around Carnoustie, it's said that nineteenth-century medical students used to seek them out in order to obtain free skeletons for their studies, and that many a hearthstone in the old Carnoustie cottages was someone's coffin lid! During the 1930s the YMCA housed a roller skating rink.

High Street, Carnoustie.

40 This view of Dundee Street was taken before 1925, when the cottage on the near right was removed to make way for the War Memorial. The ruined house opposite was replaced in 1932 by the Savings Bank. The second building on the right was the police station and the shop just past it was for some years the post office. The Co-operative Association still occupy the large shop opposite. The lane between the cottage and the police station, officially Terrace Lane, is still known as The Bobbies' Lane, although the police moved several years ago to new premises in North Burnside Street. The old police station became an old people's club called the Auld Nick!

Dundee Street, Carnoustie

41 The Cross, where Queen Street meets the High Street, is traditionally the centre of the town. The white building on the right was a shoe shop, replaced in 1926 by Dimarco's Ice Cream Parlour, a handsome Italian-style café, featuring marble and wood panelling, a glassed-in verandah and a garden where on warm days clients could eat ices and drink coffee. It was a popular meeting place and occasionally an art gallery, and many Carnoustie people mourned its passing when it was pulled down to make way for a Spar supermarket. Shortened skirts and cloche hats show how greatly fashions changed after the First World War.

The Cross, Carnoustie.

42 In this view from the other side of the Cross the domed building, typical of its architect, James Bruce, was built for William Nicoll in 1899 and contains a bakery and a restaurant. Next to it is Cross House, built for George Fairweather on the site of a cottage which housed the first Fairweather's Emporium. The brick patches on the gable show the position of fireplaces and wall cupboards, in anticipation of further building, never carried out. Note the sunblinds on the shops, supported by iron poles on the kerb.

The Cross, Carnousfie.

43   This rare picture shows the interior of Nicoll's Luncheon and Tea Rooms, scene of many a wedding reception and similar function. At the time of this photograph the restaurant is still lighted by gas. Nicoll's Bakery was famous for its cakes and patisseries. One speciality was a cup-shaped chocolate shell containing a trifle-like confection of sponge cake, jam and fruit syrup, topped with whipped cream. In later years the Tea Rooms became first a Chinese restaurant, and later a disco. At the present time they are unoccupied.

NICOLL'S LTD., CARNOUSTIE, LUNCHEON AND TEA ROOMS.

44 These Edwardian children must have been glad of a cooling paddle at a time when the accepted seaside wear for boys and girls both was the heavy serge sailor suit. Hats were essential, even when boots and stockings had been discarded. Some children are more fashionable than others . Note the natty striped blazer worn by one small boy and the tam o'shanter sported by a girl near the beach. Formal dress, including hats and gloves, was expected of mothers and governesses, even when seated on the sands. Winter's Boot and Shoe Factory can be seen in the background.

Carnoustie Beach - Wading.

45   More seaside fashion in this early version of a comic postcard. The flounced, starched and heavily-behatted beauties do not look much impressed by the chat of the young man in his up-to-the-minute outfit of flannels, striped blazer and panama hat. It's possible that the models have been photo-graphed in a studio and then super-imposed on a photo-graph of Carnoustie Links.

Carnoustie from the Links

The "beauties" here are beyond description

46 The Beach Pavilion has been a Carnoustie landmark for well over hundred years. Rather Indian in style, with its hipped roof and its verandah surrounded by decorative iron pillars, it offered teas, coffees, ices, a sheltered place to sit and a venue for summer dances. In the 1930s it was extended, rather unsympathetically, by the addition of a bathing station in that period's cubist style. The message on this card, sent in 1906 to a small boy in Buxton, explains that Lizzie, the writer, is in the crowd in front of the Pavilion taking part in a revival meeting led by a Mr. Boyd. Such seaside mission services were frequent at Carnoustie right up to the 1960s.

Carnoustie. On the Sands 2nd March Valentines Series 50001

47   By the 1920s beach-wear was less formal, but people still liked the privacy of a bathing machine for changing into swimming gear. Low tide at Carnoustie exposes a wide expanse of ribbed sand, over which these horse-drawn carriages transported their passengers to descend directly into the water. The machines were hired out by John Robb, proprietor of the Golf Inn in Park Avenue. In the early 1930s, with their wheels removed, they were lined up in front of the Beach Pavilion and rented out as changing rooms, until the opening of the Bathing Station made them redundant, and eventually they were sold off. There are still a number of them around Carnoustie, doing duty as garden sheds.

Carnoustie Beach

Valentines Series

48   Between the wars donkey rides were a popular feature of a seaside holiday. These children are possibly on an end-of-term outing, as several of them are wearing school uniforms, including their caps. The boys on the right appear to be pupils from Arbroath High School. Carnoustie Beach can be quite windy, so the square canvas structures would have provided shelter for picnickers as well as privacy for people changing into bathing costume.

On the Sands, Carnoustie

49 The Bank of Scotland on the left was built in 1880, incorporating a commodious house for the manager. No longer a bank, it now houses an interior design business. Opposite is a sign for Strachan's Garage, built in 1924. Note the Shell petrol pump at the pavement's edge, the woman carrying a petrol can, and the solitary motor car. The interesting Art Deco front of this building nowadays conceals a car park. The man on the left leading the little girl is wearing plus-fours, the popular golfing attire of the 1930s. The two girls opposite are in the height of sea-side fashion. They're wearing shorts and their shingled heads are hatless.

2630 High Street, Carnoustie.

50 The Pavilion Cinema on the right of this picture was built in 1912 to provide Carnoustie with a Public Hall suitable for theatre, concerts and cinema shows. It was roofed with corrugated iron, then a very innovative building material. It was demolished some years ago, but the rest of the street is little changed. Next to the Pavilion is the Union Hall, used during the First World War as a convalescent hospital for the war-wounded, and next again is the Golf Inn. A horse-drawn carriage is passing along the High Street, and on the right of Park Avenue a man with a ladder appears to be about to carry out some roofing work on one of the cottages.

PARK AVENUE, CARNOUSTIE.

51 This is a rare view taken from the railway bridge at the foot of Golf Street. The old cottages have the typical long gardens where the occupants used to grow vegetables and keep hens, with perhaps also a pig or a goat. This card was posted in 1912 to a man in Sydney, Australia, telling him his aunt was enjoying the sea air. The ban on sending to overseas addresses postcards with correspondence must have been lifted. However, this card bears only a one-penny stamp.

CARNOUSTIE   1238

52 Postmarked 1903, this card shows the fine Victorian houses at the east end of Carnoustie's longest street. The two with turrets are possibly James Bruce designs, while on the far left is one of Carnoustie's rare examples of 'stockbroker's Tudor'. Just beyond can be glimpsed the tower of Holyrood Episcopal Church, a scaled-down replica of the ancient Round Tower of Brechin Cathedral. This scene is little changed today, apart from the disappearance of the iron railings, removed during the Second World War. The writer of this card records that the weather on 9th July had improved after a thunderstorm the day before.

38718. IV.

MADLE STREET, CARNOUSTIE.

53 This 1902 crowd on the Links is watching the Merry Mascots concert party performing on an open-air stage. On the left Mr. Herbert Claremont can be seen at the piano. He first came to Carnoustie in 1899 as a solo busker, playing his fiddle on the beach and realised the potential for organised entertainment. He returned the following year with a team of performers to rent from the Town Council an open-air stage. In 1903 he was outbid by Gilbert Payne, who offered a higher rent for the stage. This card was sent to Miss Gordon at King's Cross Hospital, Dundee. This was the fever hospital, so perhaps her swelled face was a complication of her illness.

On the Links, Carnoustie

Dear Miss Gordon. Sorry to hear you have a swelled face hope you do not suffer from "Swelled Head"

54 Many Carnoustie home-owners who let out part or all of their houses to summer visitors had their own post-cards made by a photographer. The family from Caenlochan who stayed in 1907 in this villa near Barry Golf Club were happy to send this card to show a friend in Edinburgh their holiday home. They described it as lovely, and said they were enjoying them-selves up to the mark.

The little shop, open only during the summer months, was the official post office for Barry Camp. As well as hand-ling the military's mail, it supplied sweets and postcards to the men.

55 Political correctness was unknown when in 1907 Gilbert Payne called his concert party the White Coons. The lady is Mrs. Gilbert Payne, formerly Patty Melville, singing star of Herbert Claremont's Merry Mascots. Gilbert Payne's troupe were regulars at Carnoustie for sixteen years, performing in the open air. He offered to advance the money to build a permanent theatre, to be repaid by the Town Council over the years, but this was refused. His slogan was 'No pleasure without Payne'. Although this card was addressed to Miss Laura Ruxton in Arbroath 'from your liveing frend Evy', it has neither stamp nor postmark. Perhaps Evy wrote another card with improved spelling.

Mr. Gilbert Payne's White Coons, Carnoustie. 1907.

56 'After years of Payne, it's a time of Bliss' was the cheeky slogan of the Busy Bees, featuring Leo Bliss, his wife Dorothy Lloyd, comic Jack Hopner, whistler Percy West, and Ina Harris, George Norton, Harry Millan and Ethel Chapman. Real name Leo Amerghini, he brought his troupe to Carnoustie each year from 1916 until his death in January 1924, at the age of 40. He caught a cold as a result of playing golf in a shower of sleet, but insisted on going on stage in Manchester where he was appearing in pantomime. His cold became a fatal pneumonia. Leo had liked Carnoustie so much he named his home in Manchester Carnoustie Villa.

The Busy Bees returned to Carnoustie in May 1924 under the direction of Leo's widow, Dorothy, who continued the visits for many years.

57 In this trick photograph
Leo Bliss is both men in the
foreground. The open air
stage is lit with oil lamps. This
photograph was taken by the
author's grandfather, Robert
Luke, who produced a
number of publicity postcards
for the Busy Bees. The troupe
uniform of striped blazers
and white dresses was
changed in 1924 when Dorothy Lloyd revived the old
black and white pierrot cos-
tumes. The troupe later left
the beach to stage their per-
formances in the less exposed
Wilson's Park, beside the
Nineteenth Hole Inn in Kinloch Street. The open-air
theatre there was called Cosy
Corner.

58 The First World War marked the end of an era. Carnoustie, the town of happy family holidays and leisured golf, was suddenly very aware of the war, as train-loads of troops arrived at Barry for military training which was now very serious indeed. In this picture, taken a Barry Camp. The sheds in the foreground are where the men did their ablutions. The card was sent to his grandmother by Tommy Wilson, a young member of the Royal Engineers' Edinburgh University Training Corps. One wonders how Tommy fared in the years that followed.

Artillery entering Barry Camp.

59 The first Victoria Cross of the Great War was awarded to Carnoustie man George Jarvis, the Sapper son of Carnoustie Public School's janitor. Under heavy enemy fire he blew up a bridge at Jenappes, stopping a German advance. The other Carnoustie VC, George Samson, RNVR, gave this photograph to his former schoolmaster, John Strachan. Wounded seventeen times while carrying injured men to safety during the Gallipolli landing, Samson never fully recovered. He died of TB in the Bahamas in 1923, aged 32, and is buried there in a military cemetery. George Jarvis survived the war and later had some success as a movie actor, recreating for the cameras his bridge-demolishing exploit in a film which was shown all round Britain.

To Mr Strachan from one his old pupils G. Samson

60 After the boom years of the war, the heavy engineering industry suffered a slump. Wages were cut and overtime was stopped. This led in 1922 to the nationwide strike by the Amalgamated Engineering Union, which closed Carnoustie's Taymouth Engineering Works from March to June. Here the striking workers and their families pose outside 18 High Street, now a cycle shop, but then Mrs. Clarkson's antique shop, which appears to have supplied some of the headgear. The strikers look happy, but in the end they were forced to accept their employers' terms and had their pay reduced. James Jolly, whose name appears at the lower left-hand corner of this picture, had a confectionery and tobacco shop at 71 High Street, Carnoustie.

61 Of the more than 1,000 Carnoustie men who fought in the First World War, 142 died. The War Memorial, built on land donated by Provost George Winter, was designed by architects Bruce & Morton and dedicated on Armistice Day 1926. The statue, intended to represent the Unknown Soldier, is the work of sculptor Thomas Beattie. The model was local man Charles Crawford, of the Seaforth Highlanders, who after the war worked as a plumber in Carnoustie. The rectangular plaques bear the names of the 142 dead. A further plaque was added in the late 1940s to the front of the raised flower bed, recording the much smaller number of Second World War casualties.

WAR MEMORIAL, CARNOUSTIE.

62 This 1920s view of the beach shows people picnicking and sun-bathing among the sand dunes and marram grass which once lay between the links and the shore. Some have hired deck chairs with sun canopies. Encroachment by the tide in recent years has lead to the dunes being replaced by a sea wall with a footpath along it. Crowded beach scenes like this were normal each day throughout the summer until about thirty years ago. Since then cheap air travel and easy access to the guaranteed sunshine of Spain, Portugal and Florida has made the Carnoustie beach family holiday a thing of the past. Today's visitors are more likely to be travellers stopping off for a day while touring.

THE BEACH, CARNOUSTIE

63 Walking in and around Carnoustie was always a popular pastime with visitors and locals alike. This section of Camus Street has nowadays reverted to its old name of West Path, but it still looks much the same. The cottages, built about 1840, had to be of specified length and width and were situated at least four feet from the roadway. The walls surrounding them had to be not more than six feet in height. The walls seen here, like most in Carnoustie, are constructed of 'sea bools', round stones dug out of the sands. Several of the town's oldest houses are also constructed in whole or in part from these round stones. Beyond can be seen Agra Bank, a Georgian mansion built by Dundee ship-owner John Borrie; it is nowadays the Morven Hotel.

Camus Street, Carnoustie

64 Although the caption says Borrie's Brae, this picture is of Braehead, also called Lovers' Walk, the north-eastern end of the Terrace. Borrie's Brae, the steeply sloping road past Agra Bank, leading to West Path, lies at the foot of the steps leading down to the left. This spot has changed little, other than in the size of the trees. Of four copper beeches added in 1937 to mark the Coronation of George VI, two remain, large and healthy. Behind the wall to the right are the grounds of Carnoustie House, nowadays the town's main public park.

65 Lovers' Walk to the left and Borrie's Brae on the right have attracted a large number of strollers on this day in 1910. The photographer certainly has everyone's attention. The horse drawn vehicle is most likely a farm cart. Gladys, the writer of this card, informs her friend Yvonne that this is her favourite walk, but she did not complete Yvonne's address or post the card.

Borries Brae, Carnoustie.

Lovers' Walk and Borries Brae, Carnoustie.

66 This card is wrongly captioned, as the footpath through the Shanwell Wood was known as Lovers' Loan. It begins about 100 yards north of Lovers' Walk. This particular spot is now greatly changed as it is now the approach road to Carnoustie High School, which occupies the area to the left of this picture. The greater part of Shanwell Wood remains, and the path leading through it towards Barry is still a very popular walk. Written on the back of this postcard are the names Annie and Flo. Perhaps two of the girls in the photograph?

The Lovers Walk Carnoustie.   M. 379.

67   For the more energetic a
stroll through Panbride led to
the picturesque hollow of
Craigmill Den, then along a
path which follows the Craigmill Burn towards the bleachfield and the sea shore. Panbride Mill, glimpsed behind
the tree in the centre of the
picture, had fallen into disuse
even before a turn-of-the-cen-
tury photographer arranged
this rural scene of cow, collie,
milkmaids and lounging cyc-
list. The mill dam, however,
fed the mill lade which led to
the bleach works. Not visible
in this scene is an unusual
rock formation on the south
of the burn called the Devil's
Pulpit.

Craigmill Den, Carnoustie.

68   A little to the north of Carnoustie the Craigmill Burn passes through Batty's Den. The name may come from Patie's flax-spinning mill which operated here in the early nineteenth century, its machinery driven by water power. In 1820 the minister of Panbride, writing in the Statistical Account of Scotland, complained that the mill employed young girls who would be better at home, as their presence encouraged young men to loiter around the mill. No trace of the mill building now remains. The hump-backed bridge seen here has been replaced as the road has been widened and straightened, but Batty's Den remains a charming, leafy spot, in spring filled with primroses and wood anemones.

Batty's Den, Carnoustie.

69   The former Ladies' Golf Course has now been for many years a putting green. This 1930s picture shows rather fewer cars parked in Links Parade. The building third from the left is the Ladies' Golf Club, which has an attractive frontage with wrought-iron pillars and cameos of girls' heads. Further along can be seen the distinctive domed bay window of Simpson's Club-making workshop, which dates from 1888. The original of this picture has been hand-coloured.

PUTTING GREEN & LINKS PARADE, CARNOUSTIE

70 The first postcard with aerial views of Carnoustie went on sale in 1920. This is a little later, as it shows in the south-west corner of the Cross Dimarco's Ice Cream Parlour, built in 1926. In the immediate foreground is Winter's Boot and Shoe Factory, known as the Factory in the Garden, which produced high-quality footwear until 1958. The site is now occupied by the Lousen Park sheltered-housing complex. The dormer-windowed house second on the left from Dimarco's is First Feu Cottage, built on the site of Thomas Lowson's original dwelling. His ground extended from there to the sea, which in 1798 came much closer. 'Lousen' is the Scots spelling of the name now anglicised as Lowson.

AEROFILMS SERIES   CARNOUSTIE, FROM AN AEROPLANE   19960

71 When Miss Jean Lingard-Guthrie of Carnoustie House married Walter Reid in 1929 the former family coachman, Andrew Soutar, came out of retirement and put on his old livery to drive her to Holyrood Episcopal Church in a horse-drawn carriage hired from Innes Miller's Ferrier Street stables. Here the carriage awaits the bride in the driveway of Carnoustie House. The bride's family were the descendants of George Kinloch through the marriage of his daughter Ann with Charles Guthrie from Fife. Their daughter Helen married the Rev. Robert Lingard, who adopted his bride's surname. Carnoustie House, rebuilt in 1790 by Major Philip, was demolished some thirty years ago, after being badly damaged by fire.

72   Carnoustie's Slide was the first chute-the-chute in Scotland. When it was installed in 1929 there were complaints that adults were monopolising it. There was concern that the Slide was being used on Sundays, at a time when every Saturday night the swings had their chains wrapped round the crossbars and padlocked until Monday morning. The solution was to have a large chain made which was bolted in place the length of the Slide during the Sabbath. However, this did not deter certain Carnoustie youths from taking the risk of removing their shoes in order to slide down the chute in a standing position, straddling the chain with their stockinged feet.

THE SLIDE, CARNOUSTIE.   B.7204.

73 The often-discussed
Beach Concert Hall was given
the go-ahead in 1934 and
took just twelve weeks to
erect. It was promptly taken
by Gilbert Payne and his Jolly
Jesters. Soprano Sybil Elsie
and baritone Fred Saunders
met for the first time when
they arrived in Carnoustie,
but romance blossomed as
they sang duets. At the end of
the season, in September, a
large crowd stood outside
Carnoustie Parish Church to
cheer their wedding. Al-
though it was disparagingly
nicknamed the White Ele-
phant, the Beach Hall, now
greatly extended to include a
leisure centre, remains Carnoustie's main venue for
dances, exhibitions and large
concerts.

Beach Hall, Carnoustie   35136

74 The Paddling Pool at the mouth of the Lochty Burn was proposed in 1937 as a Coronation Year project and opened in 1938. It had a deep and a shallow end and was popular until some years ago concern about pollution from the burn which flowed through it led to its being filled in and a new pool built beside the Beach Pavilion. Not a trace of the old Paddling Pool now remains. The conical structures were stores of poles which were placed at certain seasons between high and low tidelines to support nets to trap salmon.

PADDLING POOL, CARNOUSTIE.

A.6317

75 The very popular Beach Model Railway ran for about 100 yards between the Paddling Pool and the Beach Hall. It was removed in 1941 when the beach was fortified with barbed wire and six-foot concrete blocks against possible invasion from Germany. During the war years public access to the beach through the wire was only at certain points. Landmines were laid in the War Department area of the Links and along the shore between East and Westhaven. There were some fatal accidents, including a golfer who attempted to retrieve lost balls from the minefield alongside the golf course, and a young boy who ventured into a forbidden area by the shore.

THE BEACH MODEL RAILWAY, CARNOUSTIE

76 Panbride Primary School is the oldest in Angus. It has been in the same building since 1815. The infants' class of 1908, with their teacher, Miss Violet Scott, look awed by the camera. Many of the Eton collars worn by the boys were made of spongeable rubber. Embroidered and starched pinafores were normal wear for girls. At the time of this picture Panbride School had over three hundred pupils aged from four to fourteen. They were served a mid-day meal of soup for which a Carnoustie butcher donated bones and local farmers the vegetables. Scholars who could afford it paid one penny for the first bowl and a halfpenny for 'seconds'. Children from poor families had their soup free.

77 Fourteen years later school wear was much less formal, although the boy at the extreme left of the back row is wearing a kilt outfit in this picture of Barry School's Standard Five in 1922. The Qualifying Examination taken in Standard Five decided whether scholars stayed on for Standard Six or left for higher education at either the Grove Academy in Broughty Ferry or the High School of Arbroath. Standard Six instruction was practical rather than academic.

78 These Standard Six boys at Barry School in 1912 are having a woodwork lesson with Mr. John Strachan, just visible at the back of the room. They would leave school at the age of thirteen or fourteen, most of them to work on the land as farm servants. Other possibilities of employment were in Anderson's Engineering Works, or as apprentices in plumbing, carpentry or house painting. Girls could seek posts as domestic servants, or in Smieton's Works, where jute had now replaced linen, or in one of the town's two shoemaking factories.

79 At the beginning of the Dundee Trades Holiday Fortnight in July 1927 the young daughters of the Luke family invited friends to join them for tea on the lawn outside their holiday cottage in Terrace Road, Carnoustie. Jean Luke, in the white hat in the foreground, was a dressmaker with Maison Soutar of Dundee. Several of the guests are her colleagues. Holding the kettles are her sisters Bertha and Margaret. Annie is concealed by the tree in front of the cottage door.
Robert Luke, a Dundee clerk, rented both a flat in the city and a cottage in Carnoustie, where the family spent weekends and school holidays.

80 Brothers David and Edgar Thompson, of Greenlawhill Farm, Barry, built this farm cart themselves in 1927. With horse Roy between the shafts they're about to take some of the family for a trip. The small boy in the bus conductor's uniform is Edgar's son, Billy, then aged four. With him are his grandmother, mother and young aunts. Note the neatly thatched corn-stacks covered with netting to protect them from the wind.

81 The fishing village of Westhaven, now part of Carnoustie, is older than the rest of the town. Nowadays only hobby fishing is carried on, but at the time of this picture there were still working fishermen whose wives had the task of baiting the lines with shellfish. The woman is wearing the traditional Angus fishwife's costume of drugget petticoat, striped apron, print blouse and starched linen mutch. With its picturesque cottages and natural harbour, Westhaven was a favourite spot with artists such as William MacTaggart.

82 Following the Disruption of the Church of Scotland in 1843 the Rev. James Lumsden and many of his congregation left the established Kirk to form Barry Free Church. After for some months meeting in a disused plash mill, they built a small, cottage-like chapel on land belonging to Greenlawhill Farm. In 1888, owing to the rapid growth of Carnoustie this was replaced by the present Barry Church, designed by James McLaren. The two Barry churches were united in 1953, and the older church was some years later closed and then demolished. The house on the left of this picture now has an upper storey. Just visible on the left is part of the minister's stable, now converted into a house.

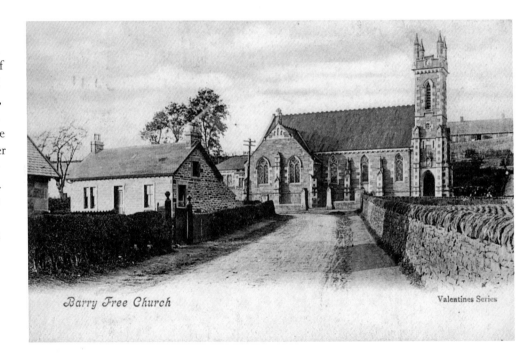

Barry Free Church

Valentines Series